I0011479

Book 1
C++ Programming Professional Made Easy

BY SAM KEY

&

Book 2
MYSQL Programming Professional Made Easy

BY SAM KEY

Book 1
C++ Programming Professional Made Easy

BY SAM KEY

Expert C++ Programming Language Success in a Day for Any Computer User!

Programming Box Set #60: C++ Programming Professional Made Easy & MySQL Programming Professional Made Easy

Programming Box Set #60: C++ Programming Professional Made Easy & MySQL Programming Professional Made Easy

Table Of Contents

Introduction

I want to thank you and congratulate you for purchasing the book, "Professional C++ Programming Made Easy".

This book contains proven steps and strategies on how to learn the C++ programming language as well as its applications.

There's no need to be a professional developer to code quick and simple C++ programs. With this book, anyone with basic computer knowledge can explore and enjoy the power of the *C++ Programming Language*. Included are the following fundamental topics for any beginner to start coding *today:*

- The basic C++ terms
- Understanding the C++ Program Structure
- Working with Variables, Expressions, and Operators
- Using the Input and Output Stream for User Interaction
- Creating Logical Comparisons
- Creating Loops and Using Condition Statements
- And Many More!

Thanks again for purchasing this book, I hope you enjoy it!

Chapter 1 – Introduction to C++

What You Will Learn:

****A Brief History of the C++ Language*

****C++ Basic Terminology*

****C++ Program Structure*

C++ is one of the most popular programming languages that people are using today. More specifically, C++ is a library of "commands" that tell your computer what to do and how to do it. These commands make up the *C++ source code.*

Take note that C++ is different from the *C* programming language that came before it. In fact, it is supposedly better version of the C language when *Bjarne Stroustrup* created it back in 1983.

Even today, the C++ language serves as the "starting point" for many experts in the world of programming. Although it is particularly easy to learn and apply, the ceiling for C++ mastery is incredibly high.

C++ Basic Terminology

Of course, the first step in learning the C++ programming language is to understand the basic terms. To prevent any unnecessary confusion at any point as you read this book, this section explains the most commonly used terms in the C++ program syntax. Just like the entire programming language itself, most terms in C++ are easy to remember and understand.

Compiler

Before anything else, take note that a compiler is needed to run the codes you've written with C++. Think of compilers as "translators" that convert programming language into *machine language* – the language that a computer understands. The machine language consists of only two characters (1s and 0s), which is why it is also called as *binary language*. If you're learning C++ at school, then you shouldn't worry about getting a compiler for C++ *or* an *Integrated Development Environment* for that matter.

Integrated Development Environment

An Integrated Development Environment (IDE) is essentially the software you're using to write C++ programs. It only makes sense for IDEs to come with compilers needed to run your codes. If you have no experience with C++ programming and attempting to learn it on your own, you can opt for a free C++ IDE such as *Code::Blocks*. A good choice for complete beginners is to opt for a simple C++ IDE such as *Quincy 2005* since there is very little setup required.

Variables and Parameters

Variables are individual blocks in the program's memory that contains a given value. A value may be set as a constant, determined by the value of other variables using operators, or set/changed through user input. Variables are denoted by variable names or *identifiers*. In programming with C++, you can use any variable name you desire as long as all characters are valid. Remember that only alphanumeric characters and "underscores" (_) can be used in identifiers. Punctuation marks and other symbols are not allowed.

Keep in mind that variables always need to be *declared* first before they can be used. Declaring variables are different from deciding their actual values; meaning both processes are done in two different codes. These processes will be explained in the next chapter.

"Parameters" work the same way as regular variables. In fact, they are even written in the same syntax. However, parameters and variables are initialized in different ways. Parameters are specifically included in *functions* to allow arguments to be passed to a separate location from which the functions are called.

Statements

Every program written with C++ consists of different lines of code that performs tasks such as setting variables, calling functions, and other expressions. These lines are *statements*. Each individual statement always ends with a semicolon (;). More importantly, statements in a function are executed chronologically based on which comes first. Of course, this order can be altered using *flow control statements* such as "if statements" and "loops".

Functions

Functions are blocks in a C++ program structured to complete a single task. You can call upon functions at any point whilst the program is running. Curly brackets or braces ({}) enclose the statements or "body" in each function. Aside from a function name, functions are also set with corresponding "types" which refer to the requested form of *returned value*. You can also use and set parameters at the beginning of each function. They are enclosed in parentheses "()" and separated using commas (,).

In C++, the following is the most used syntax when creating functions:

```
"type" "name" ( parameter 1, parameter 2, parameter 3, ...)
{
        "statements";
}
```

Comments

When working on particularly bigger projects, most experienced programmers use "comments" that can be used as descriptions for specific sections in a C++ program. Comments are completely ignored by a compiler and can therefore ignore proper coding syntax. Comments are preceded either by a *two slashes* (//) or a *slash-asterisk* (/*). You will find comments in the examples throughout this book to help you understand them. A quick example would be the "*Hello World!*" program below. Of course, you can also use comments in your future projects for reference and debugging purposes.

The C++ Program Structure

The program structure of C++ is very easy to understand. The compiler reads every line of code from top to bottom. This is why the first part of a C++ program usually starts with *preprocessor directives* and the declaration of variables and their values. The best way to illustrate this structure is to use the most popular example in the world of C++ -- the "Hello World!" program. Take note of the lines of code as well as the comments below:

#include <iostream> // this is a preprocessor directive

int main() // this line initiates the function named main, which should be found in every C++ program

{

> **std::cout << "Hello World!";** // the statements found between the curly braces make up the main function's body
>
> **return 0;** // the return 0; statement is required to tell the program that the function ran correctly. However, some compilers do not require this line in the main function

}

The topmost line ("#include <iostream>") is a preprocessor directive that defines a section of the standard C++ programming library known as the Input/Output Stream or simply *iostream.* This section handles the input and output operations in C++ programs. Remember that this is important if you wish to use "std::cout" in the main function's body.

The first line "int main ()" initializes the main function. Remember that the "int" refers to the *integer* data type and he "main" refers to the function's name. There are other data types aside from int. But you should focus on the integer data type for now. Since the "Hello World!" program does not need a parameter, it leaves the space between the parentheses succeeding the function name blank. Also, bear in mind that you should NOT place a semicolon (;) after initializing functions.

Next is the function's body, denoted by the open curly brace. This particular part ("std::cout") of the program refers to the **st**andar**d** **c**haracter **out**put device, which is the computer's display device. Next comes the *insertion operator* (<<) from the input/output stream which means the rest of the line is to be outputted (excluding quotations). Lastly, the statement is closed with a semicolon (;).

The last line in the function's body is the *return statement* ("return = 0;"). Remember that the return expression (in this example, "0") depends on the data type specified upon initialization of the function. However, it is possible to create functions without the need for return statements using the "void" function type. For example; *void main ().*

An alternate way to do this is to include the line "using namespace std;" under the preprocessor line so you no longer need to write "std::" each time you use it. If you opt for this method, the code would look like:

```
#include <iostream>

using namespace std;

int main()

{

    cout << "Hello World!";

    return 0;

}
```

Chapter 2 – C++ Variables and Operators

What You Will Learn:

***Introduction to C++ Operators and How to Use Them*

***Declaring and Determining the Value of Variables*

***Creating New Lines in the Program Output*

In a C++ program, variables and constants are controlled or "operated" using *Operators.* Take note that the basic operators in the C++ programming language are essentially the same as arithmetic operator. This includes the equal sign (=) for assigning expressions, the plus sign (+) for addition, the minus sign (-) for subtraction, the asterisk (*) for multiplication, the forward slash (/) for division, and the percentage sign (%) for obtaining the remainder from any expression.

C++ also uses other operators to fulfill additional tasks other than basic arithmetic operations. As mentioned in the previous chapter, the iostream header allowed you to use the insertion operator (<<) for processing output. There are also different operators accessible even without the #include directive. These "basic" operators can be categorized under *increment/decrement operators, comparison operators, compound assignment operators,* and *logical operators.*

Declaring Variables

Before using variables in C++ operations, you must first declare them and determine their values. Again, declaring variables and giving their values are two separate processes. The syntax for declaring variables are as follows:

"type" "variable";

Just like when initializing functions, you need to specify the data type to be used for a given variable. For example; say you want to declare "x" as an integer variable. The initialization should look like this:

int x;

After the declaration of x, you can give it a value using the assign operator (=). For example; to assign the value "99" to variable x, use the following line:

x = 99;

Make sure to declare a variable first before you assign a value to it. Alternatively, you can declare a variable and assign a value to it using a single line. This can be done using:

int x = 99;

Aside from setting these expressions as you write the program, you can also use operations and user input to determine their values as the program runs. But first, you need to learn about the other operators in C++.

Increment and Decrement Operators

The increment operator consists of two plus signs (++) while the decrement operator consists of two minus signs (--). The main purpose of increment and decrement operators is to shorten the expression of adding and subtracting 1 from any given variable. For example; if x = 2, then ++x should equal 3 while –x should equal 1.

If being used to determine the values of two or more variables, increment and decrement operators can be included as either a prefix or suffix. When used as a suffix (x++ or x--), it denotes the original value of x *before* adding or subtracting 1. When run on their own, both ++x and x++ have the same meaning. But when used in setting other variables, the difference is made obvious. Here is a simple example to illustrate the difference:

X = 5;

Y = ++x;

In this example, the value of y is determined *after* increasing the value of x. In other words, the value of y in this example is equal to 6.

X = 5;

Y = x++;

In this example, the value of y is determined *before* increasing the value of x. In other words, the value of y in this example is equal to 6.

Compound Assignment Operators

Aside from basic arithmetic operators and the standard assignment operator (=), compound assignment operators can also be used to perform an operation before a value is assigned. Compound assignment operators are basically shortened versions of normal expressions that use basic arithmetic operators.

Here are some examples of compound assignment operators:

```
x -= 1; // this is the same as the expression x = x – 1;

x *= y; // this is the same as the expression x = x * y;

x += 1;         // this is the same as the expression x = x + 1;

x /= y;         // this is the same as the expression x = x / y;
```

Comparison Operators

Variables and other expressions can be compared using relational or comparison operators. These operators are used to check whether a value is greater than, less than, or equal to another. Here are the comparison operators used in C++ and their description:

==	-	checks if the values are equal
<	-	checks if the first value is less than the second
>	-	checks if the first value is greater than the second

<=	-	checks if the first value is less than *or* equal to the second
>=	-	checks if the first value is greater than *or* equal to the second
!=	-	checks if the values are NOT equal

Comparison operators are commonly used in creating condition statements. They can also be used to evaluate an expression and return a *Boolean value* ("true" or "false"). Using the comparison operators listed above; here are some example expressions and their corresponding Boolean value:

```
(8 == 1) // this line evaluates to "false"
(8 > 1)  // this line evaluates to "true"
(8 != 1) // this line evaluates to "true"
(8 <= 1) // this line evaluates to "false"
```

Also take note that the Boolean value "false" is equivalent to "0" while "true" is equivalent to other non-zero integers.

Aside from numerical values, the value of variables can also be checked when using comparison operators. Simply use a variable's identifier when creating the expression. Of course, the variable must be declared and given an identified value first before a valid comparison can be made. Here is an example scenario

```
#include <iostream>
using namespace std;

int main ()

{
        int a = 3;      // the values of a and b are set first
        int b = 4;
        cout << "Comparison a < b = " << (a < b);
        return 0;
}
```

The output for this code is as follows:

Comparison a < b = true

Take note that the insertion operator (<<) is used to insert the value of the expression "a < b" in the output statement, which is denoted in the 7th line ("cout << "Comparison a < b = "...). Don't forget that you *need an output statement* in order to see if your code works. The following code will produce no errors, but it won't produce an output either:

```
#include <iostream>

int main (

{
        int a = 3;
        int b = 4;
        (a < b);
        return 0;
}
```

In this code, it is also true that a < b. However, no output will be produced since the lines necessary for the program output are omitted.

Logical Operators

There are also other logical operators in C++ that can determine the values of Boolean data. They are the NOT (!), AND (&&), and OR (||) operators. Here are specific examples on how they are used:

!(6 > 2) // the **NOT** operator (!) completely reverses any relational expressions and produces the opposite result. This expression is false because 6 > 2 is correct

(6 > 2 && 5 < 10) // the **AND** (&&) operator only produces true if both expressions correct. This expression is true because both 6 > 2 && 5 < 10 are correct

(6 = 2 || 5 < 10) // the **OR** (||) operator produces true if one of the expressions are correct. This expression is true because the 5 < 10 is correct although 6 = 2 is false.

You can also use the NOT operator in addition to the other two logical operators. For example:

!(6 = 2 || 5 < 10) // this expression is false

!(6 > 2 && 5 < 10) // this expression is also false

!(6 < 2 && 5 < 10) // this expression is true

Creating New Lines

From this point on in this book, you will be introduced to simple C++ programs that produce output with multiple lines. To create new lines when producing output, all you need to do is to use the *new line character* (\n). Alternatively, you can use the "endl;" manipulator to create new lines when using the "cout" code. The main difference is that the *internal buffer* for the output stream is "flushed" whenever you use the "endl;" manipulator with "cout". Here are examples on how to use both:

cout << "Sentence number one \nSentence number two";

The example above uses the new line character.

cout << "Sentence number one" << endl;
cout << "Sentence number two";

The example above uses "endl;".

Of course, the first code (using \n) is relatively simpler and easier for general output purposes. Both will produce the following output:

Sentence number one

Sentence number two

Chapter 3 – All About User Input

What You Will Learn:

***Utilizing the Input Stream*

***Using Input to Determine or Modify Values*

***How to Input and Output Strings*

Up to this point, you've learned how to make a C++ program that can perform arithmetic operations, comparisons, and can produce output as well. This time, you will learn how to code one of the most important aspects of computer programs – *user input.*

As stated earlier, user input can be utilized to determine or modify the values of certain variables. C++ programs use abstractions known as *streams* to handle input and output. Since you already know about the syntax for output ("cout"), it's time to learn about the syntax for input ("cin").

The Extraction Operator

The input syntax "cin" is used with the *extraction operator* (>>) for formatted input. This combination along with the *keyboard* is the standard input for most program environments. Remember that you still need to declare a variable first before input can be made. Here is a simple example:

int x; // this line declares the variable identifier x. Take note of the data type "int" which means that only an integer value is accepted

cin >> x; // this line extracts input from the cin syntax and stores it to x

User input can also be requested for multiple variables in a single line. For example; say you want to store integer values for variables x and y. This should look like:

```
int x, y;        // this line declares the two variables

cin >> x >> y;        // this line extracts user input for variables x and y
```

Take note that the program will automatically require the user to input *two* values for the two variables. Which comes first depends on the order of the variables in the line (in this case, input for variable "x" is requested first).

Here is an example of a program that extracts user input and produces an output:

```
#include <iostream>     // again, this is essential for input and output
using namespace std;

int main ()

{
        int x;
        cout << "Insert a random number \n";
        cin >> x;      // this is where user input is extracted
        cout << "You inserted: " << x;
        return 0;

}
```

Bear in mind that the value extracted from the input stream overwrites any initial value of a variable. For example, if the variable was declared as "int x = 2;" but was later followed by the statement "cin >> x;", the new value will then replace the original value until the program/function restarts or if an assignment statement is introduced.

Strings

Keep in mind that there are other types you can assign to variables in C++. Aside from integers, another fundamental type is the *string*. A string is basically a variable type that can store sets of characters in a specific sequence. In other words, this is how you can assign words or sentences as values for certain variables.

First of all, you need to add the preprocessor directive "#include <string>" before you can use strings in your program. Next, you need to declare a string before it can receive assignments. For example; if you want to declare a string for "Name" and assign a value for it, you can use the code:

```
#include <string>
using namespace std;

int main ()

{
  string name;
  name =  "Insert your name here"; // including quotations

}
```

Creating output using strings is basically the same as with integers. You only need to use "cout" and insert the string to the line. The correct syntax is as follows:

```
string name;

Name = "Your Name Here";

cout << "My name is: " << name;
```

Without any changes, the output for the above code is:

Your Name Here

Inputting Strings

To allow user input values for strings, you need to use the function "getline" in addition to the standard input stream "cin". The syntax for this is "getline (cin, [string]);". Below is an example program that puts string input into application.

```
#include <iostream>
#include <string>
using namespace std;

int main ()

{
        string name;
        cout << "Greetings! What is your name?\n";
        getline (cin, name); // this is the extraction syntax
        cout << "Welcome " << name;
        return 0;

}
```

Take note that strings have "blank" values by default. This means nothing will be printed if no value is assigned or if there is no user input.

Chapter 4 – Using Flow Control Statements

What You Will Learn:

***If and Else Selection Statements*

***Creating Choices*

***Creating Iterating/Looping Statements*

Remember that statements are the basic building blocks of a program written using C++. Each and every line that contains expressions such as a variable declaration, an operation, or an input extraction is a statement.

However, these statements are *linear* without some form of flow control that can establish the "sense" or "logic" behind a C++ program. This is why you should learn how to utilize flow control statements such as *selection statements* and *looping statements.*

If and Else Statements

If and else statements are the most basic form of logic in a C++ program. Basically, the main purpose of an "if" statement is to allow the execution of a specific line or "block" of multiple statements only *if* a specified condition is fulfilled.

Next is the "else" statement which allows you to specify what would occur in case the conditions aren't met. Without an "else" statement, everything inside the "if" statement will be completely ignored. Here the syntax for an "if" and "else" statement:

```
if (age >= 18)
        cout << "You are allowed to drink.";
```

```
else
        cout << "You are not yet allowed to drink.";
```

Remember that conditions can only be set using comparison operators and logical operators (refer to Chapter 2). Take note that you can also execute multiple statements using if/else conditions by enclosing the lines in curly braces. It is also possible to use composite conditions using logical operators such as AND (&&) and OR (||).

Finally, you can use another "if" statement after an "else" statement for even more possibilities. Of course, you also need to specify conditions for every "if" statement you use. Here is a good example that demonstrates what you can do using "if" and "else" statements in addition to user input:

```
#include <iostream>
using namespace std;

int main()

{
        int number;
        cout << "Enter a number from 1-3\n";
        cin >> number;
        if (number == 1 || number == 2)
                cout << "You have entered either 1 or 2.";
        else if (number == 3)
                cout << "You have entered 3.";
        else
        {
                cout << "Please follow the instructions\n";
                cout << "Please Try Again.";
        }
        return 0;
}
```

There are 3 possible outcomes in the program above. The first outcome is achieved if the user entered any of the numbers 1 or 2. The second outcome is achieved if the user entered the number 3. Lastly, the third outcome is achieved if the user entered a different number other the ones specified.

Creating Choices (Yes or No)

Another way to utilize if/else statements is to create "Yes or No" choices. For this, you need to make use of the variable type "char" which can hold a character from the *8-bit character set* (you can use char16_t, char32_t, or wchar_t for larger character sets; but this is not usually necessary). Just like all other variables, a "char" variable needs to be declared before it can be used.

Of course, you want the user to make the choice, which is why you need to use the "cin" function to extract user input. Here is a simple program that asks for the user's gender:

```
#include <iostream>
using namespace std;

int main()

{
        char gender; // this is the char variable declaration
        cout << "Male or Female? (M/F)";
        cin >> gender; // user input is stored to gender
        if (gender == 'm' || gender == 'M')
                cout << "You have selected Male.";
        else if (gender == 'f' || gender == 'F')
                cout << "You have selected Female.";
        else
                cout << "Please follow the instructions.";
        return 0;

}
```

Take note that you should use *single quotation marks* (') when pinpointing "char" values. In C++, "char" values are always called inside single quotation marks. Additionally, remember that "char" values are case-sensitive, which is why the example above used the OR (||) operator in the conditions to accept both lowercase and uppercase answers. You can see that the program above checked if the user entered 'm', 'M', 'f', or 'F'.

Looping Statements

Lastly, using "loops" allow statements to be executed for a set number of times or until a condition is met. By incorporating other statements in loops, you can do far more than just create pointless repetitions. But first, you need to be familiar with the different types of loops.

There are 3 types of loops in C++ -- *while, do,* and *for.*

While Loop

The *"while loop"* is regarded as the simplest form of loop in the C++. Basically, it repeats the statement(s) as long as the given condition is true. Keep in mind that your code should be structured to eventually fulfill the condition; otherwise you might create an "infinite loop".

Here is an example of a while loop:

```
int x = 100;

while (x >= 0)      // the condition for the loop is set
    {
    cout << x;
    --x;    // the value of x is decreased
    }
```

In this example, the loop executes as long as the value of x is greater than or equal to 0. Take note of the decrement operator (--) in the statement "--x;". This makes sure that the value of x is continually decreased until the condition is met and the loop ends.

Do-While Loop

The next type of loop is the "*do-while loop*". The do-while loop is essentially the same as the while loop. The main difference is that the do-while loop allows the execution of the statement(s) at least *once* before the condition is checked. Whereas in the while loop, the condition is checked *first.*

Here is an example of a do-while loop:

```
int x = 100;
int y;

do
    {
    cout << "The value is " << x << "\n";
    cout << "Enter a value to subtract.";
    cin >> y;
    x -= y;
    }
while (x > 0);       // in the do-while loop, the condition is checked last
```

In the example above, the statements are executed at least once before the value of x is checked. Whereas in a while loop, there is a possibility that the statement(s) will not be executed at all.

For Loop

The third type of loop is the *"for loop"* which has specific areas for the *initialization, condition,* and *increase.* These three sections are sequentially executed throughout the life cycle of the loop. By structure, for loops are created to run a certain number of times because increment or decrement operators are usually used in the "increase" section.

Here is the syntax for this loop to help you understand it better:

```
for (int x = 10; x > 0; x--)
```

Notice the three expressions inside the parentheses (int x = 10; x > 0; x--) are separated in semicolons. These parameters denote the three sections of the loop. You may also use multiple expressions for each section using a comma (,). Here is the syntax for this:

```
for ( int x = 10, y = 0; x != y; --x, ++y )
        {
        cout << "X and Y is different\n";
        }
```

In this example, the loop is executed as long as x is not equal to y. And in order for the loop to end, the values of x and y are adjusted until the value of x equals the value of y. Based on the parameters above, the statement "X and Y is different" will run a total of 5 times before the loop is ended.

Conclusion

Thank you again for purchasing this book!

I hope this book was able to help you to learn and understand the C++ programming language!

The next step is to start from where you are now and try to learn something new. Keep in mind that you've only scratched the surface of all the things you can do in the world of C++!

Finally, if you enjoyed this book, please take the time to share your thoughts and post a review on Amazon. We do our best to reach out to readers and provide the best value we can. Your positive review will help us achieve that. It'd be greatly appreciated!

Thank you and good luck!

Book 2
MYSQL Programming Professional Made Easy

BY SAM KEY

Expert MYSQL Programming Language Success in a Day for any Computer User!

Programming Box Set #60: C++ Programming Professional Made Easy & MySQL Programming Professional Made Easy

Table Of Contents

Introduction

I want to thank you and congratulate you for purchasing the book, "MYSQL Programming Professional Made Easy: Expert MYSQL Programming Language Success in a Day for any Computer User!".

This book contains proven steps and strategies on how to manage MySQL databases.

The book will teach you the fundamentals of SQL and how to apply it on MySQL. It will cover the basic operations such as creating and deleting tables and databases. Also, it will tell you how to insert, update, and delete records in MySQL. In the last part of the book, you will be taught on how to connect to your MySQL server and send queries to your database using PHP.

Thankfully, by this time, this subject is probably a piece of cake for you since you might already have experienced coding in JavaScript and PHP, which are prerequisites to learning MySQL.

However, it does not mean that you will have a difficult time learning MySQL if you do not have any idea on those two scripting languages. In this book, you will learn about SQL, which works a bit different from programming languages.

Being knowledgeable alone with SQL can give you a solid idea on how MySQL and other RDBMS work. Anyway, thanks again for purchasing this book, I hope you enjoy it!

Chapter 1: Introduction to MySQL

This book will assume that you are already knowledgeable about PHP. It will focus on database application on the web. The examples here will use PHP as the main language to use to access a MySQL database. Also, this will be focused on Windows operating system users.

As of now, MySQL is the most popular database system by PHP programmers. Also, it is the most popular database system on the web. A few of the websites that use MySQL to store their data are Facebook, Wikipedia, and Twitter.

Commonly, MySQL databases are ran on web servers. Because of that, you need to use a server side scripting language to use it.

A few of the good points of MySQL against other database systems are it is scalable (it is good to use in small or large scale applications), fast, easy to use, and reliable. Also, if you are already familiar with SQL, you will not have any problems in manipulating MySQL databases.

Preparation

In the first part of this book, you will learn SQL or Standard Query Language. If you have a database program, such as Microsoft Access, installed in your computer, you can use it to practice and apply the statements you will learn.

In case you do not, you have two options. Your first option is to get a hosting account package that includes MySQL and PHP. If you do not want to spend tens of dollars for a paid web hosting account, you can opt for a free one. However, be informed that most of them will impose limitations or add annoyances, such as ads, in your account. Also, some of them have restrictions that will result to your account being banned once you break one of them.

Your second option is to get XAMMP, a web server solution that includes Apache, MySQL, and PHP. It will turn your computer into a local web server. And with it, you can play around with your MySQL database and the PHP codes you want to experiment with. Also, it comes with phpMyAdmin. A tool that will be discussed later in this book.

Chapter 2: Database and SQL

What is a database? A database is an application or a file wherein you can store data. It is used and included in almost all types of computer programs. A database is usually present in the background whether the program is a game, a word processor, or a website.

A database can be a storage location for a player's progress and setting on a game. It can be a storage location for dictionaries and preferences in word processors. And it can be a storage location for user accounts and page content in websites.

There are different types and forms of databases. A spreadsheet can be considered a database. Even a list of items in a text file can be considered one, too. However, unlike the database that most people know or familiar with, those kinds of databases are ideal for small applications.

RDBMS

The type of database that is commonly used for bigger applications is RDBMS or relational database management system. MySQL is an RDBMS. Other RDBMS that you might have heard about are Oracle database, Microsoft Access, and SQL Server.

Inside an RDBMS, there are tables that are composed of rows, columns, and indexes. Those tables are like spreadsheets. Each cell in a table holds a piece of data. Below is an example table:

username	*password*	*email*	*firstname*	*lastname*
Johnnyxxx	*123abc*	*jjxxx@gmail.com*	*Johnny*	*Stew*
cutiepatutie	*qwertyuiop*	*cuteme@yahoo.com*	*Sara*	*Britch*
mastermiller	*theGear12*	*mgshades@gmail.com*	*Master*	*Miller*
j_sasaki	*H9fmaNCa*	*j_sasaki@gmail.com*	*Johnny*	*Sasaki*

Note: this same table will be used as the main reference of all the examples in this book. Also, developers usually encrypt their passwords in their databases. They are not encrypted for the sake of an example.

In the table, which the book will refer to as the account table under the sample database, there are six columns (or fields) and they are id, username, password, email, firstname, and lastname. As of now, there are only four rows. Rows can be also called entries or records. Take note that the first row is not part of the count. They are just there to represent the name of the columns as headers.

An RDBMS table can contain one or more tables.

Compared to other types of databases, RDBMS are easier to use and manage because it comes with a standardized set of method when it comes to accessing and manipulating data. And that is SQL or Standard Query Language.

SQL

Before you start learning MySQL, you must familiarize yourself with SQL or Standard Query Language first. SQL is a language used to manipulate and access relational database management systems. It is not that complicated compared to learning programming languages.

Few of the things you can do with databases using SQL are:

- Get, add, update, and delete data from databases
- Create, modify, and delete databases
- Modify access permissions in databases

Most database programs use SQL as the standard method of accessing databases, but expect that some of them have a bit of variations. Some statements have different names or keywords while some have different methods to do things. Nevertheless, most of the usual operations are the same for most of them.

A few of the RDBMS that you can access using SQL – with little alterations – are MySQL, SQL Server, and Microsoft Access.

Chapter 3: SQL Syntax

SQL is like a programming language. It has its own set of keywords and syntax rules. Using SQL is like talking to the database. With SQL, you can pass on commands to the database in order for it to present and manipulate the data it contains for you. And you can do that by passing queries and statements to it.

SQL is commonly used interactively in databases. As soon as you send a query or statement, the database will process it immediately. You can perform some programming in SQL, too. However, it is much easier to leave the programming part to other programming languages. In the case of MySQL, it is typical that most of the programming is done with PHP, which is the most preferred language to use with it.

SQL's syntax is simple. Below is an example:

```
SELECT username FROM account
```

In the example, the query is commanding the database to get all the data under the username column from the account table. The database will reply with a recordset or a collection of records.

In MySQL, databases will also return the number of rows it fetched and the duration that it took to fetch the result.

Case Sensitivity

As you can see, the SQL query is straightforward and easy to understand. Also, take note that unlike PHP, MySQL is not case sensitive. Even if you change the keyword SELECT's case to select, it will still work. For example:

```
seLeCT username from account
```

However, as a standard practice, it is best that you type keywords on uppercase and values in lowercase.

Line Termination

In case that you will perform or send consecutive queries or a multiline query, you need to place a semicolon at the end of each statement to separate them. By the way, MySQL does not consider a line to be a statement when it sees a new line character – meaning, you can place other parts of your queries on multiple lines. For example:

```
SELECT
```

username

FROM

account;

New lines are treated like a typical whitespace (spaces and tabs) character. And the only accepted line terminator is a semicolon. In some cases, semicolons are not needed to terminate a line.

Chapter 4: SQL Keywords and Statements

When you memorize the SQL keywords, you can say that you are already know SQL or MySQL. Truth be told, you will be mostly using only a few SQL keywords for typical database management. And almost half of the queries you will be making will be SELECT queries since retrieving data is always the most used operation in databases.

Before you learn that, you must know how to create a database first.

CREATE DATABASE

Creating a database is simple. Follow the syntax below:

CREATE DATABASE <name of database>;

To create the sample database where the account table is located, this is all you need to type:

CREATE DATABASE sample;

Easy, right? However, an empty database is a useless database. You cannot enter any data to it yet since you do not have tables yet.

CREATE TABLE

Creating a table requires a bit of planning. Before you create a table, you must already know the columns you want to include in it. Also, you need to know the size, type, and other attributes of the pieces of data that you will insert on your columns. Once you do, follow the syntax below:

CREATE TABLE <name of table>

(

<name of column 1> <data type(size)> <attributes>,

<name of column 2> <data type(size)> <attributes>,

<name of column 3> <data type(size)> <attributes>

);

By the way, you cannot just create a table out of nowhere. To make sure that the table you will create will be inside a database, you must be connected to one.

Connection to databases will be discussed in the later part of this book. As of now, imagine that you are now connected to the sample database that was just created in the previous section.

To create the sample account table, you need to do this:

```
CREATE TABLE account

(

id int(6) PRIMARY KEY UNSIGNED AUTO_INCREMENT PRIMARY KEY,

username varchar(16),

password varchar(16),

email varchar(32),

firstname var(16),

lastname var(16),

);
```

The example above commands the database to create a table named account. Inside the parentheses, the columns that will be created inside the account table are specified. They are separated with a comma. The first column that was created was the id column.

According to the example, the database needs to create the id column (id). It specified that the type of data that it will contain would be integers with six characters (int(6)). Also, it specified some optional attributes. It said that the id column will be the PRIMARY KEY of the table and its values will AUTO_INCREMENT – these will be discussed later. Also, it specified that the integers or data under it will be UNSIGNED, which means that only positive integers will be accepted.

MySQL Data Types

As mentioned before, databases or RDBMS accept multiple types of data. To make databases clean, it is required that you state the data type that you will input in your table's columns. Aside from that, an RDBMS also needs to know the size of the data that you will enter since it will need to allocate the space it needs to store the data you will put in it. Providing precise information about the size of your data will make your database run optimally.

Below are some of the data types that you will and can store in a MySQL database:

- INT(size) – integer data type. Numbers without fractional components or decimal places. A column with an INT data type can accept any number between -2147483648 to 2147483648. In case that you specified that it will be UNSIGNED, the column will accept any number between 0 to 4294967295. You can specify the number of digits with INT. The maximum is 11 digits – it will include the negative sign (-).
- FLOAT(size, decimal) – float data type. Numbers with fractional components or decimal places. It cannot be UNSIGNED. You can specify the number of digits it can handle and the number of decimal places it will store. If you did not specify the size and number of decimals, MySQL will set it to 10 digits and 2 decimal places (the decimal places is included in the count of the digits). Float can have the maximum of 24 digits.
- TIME – time will be stored and formatted as HH:MM:SS.
- DATE – date will be stored and formatted as YYYY-MM-DD. It will not accept any date before year 1,000. And it will not accept date that exceeds 31 days and 12 months.
- DATETIME – combination of DATE and TIME formatted as YYYY-MM-DD HH:MM:SS.
- TIMESTAMP – formatted differently from DATETIME. Its format is YYYYMMDDHHMMSS. It can only store date and time between 19700101000000 and 20371231235959 (not accurate).
- CHAR(size) – stores strings with fixed size. It can have a size of 1 to 255 characters. It uses static memory allocation, which makes it perform faster than VARCHAR. It performs faster because the database will just multiply its way to reach the location of the data you want instead of searching every byte to find the data that you need. To make the data fixed length, it is padded with spaces after the last character.
- VARCHAR(size) – stores strings with variable length size. It can have a size of 1 to 255 characters. It uses dynamic memory allocation, which is slower than static. However, when using VARCHAR, it is mandatory to specify the data's size.
- BLOB –store BLOBs (Binary Large Objects). Data is stored as byte strings instead of character strings (in contrast to TEXT). This makes it possible to store images, documents, or other files in the database.
- TEXT – store text with a length of 65535 characters or less.
- ENUM(x, y, z) – with this, you can specify the values that can be only stored.

INT, BLOB, and TEXT data types can be set smaller or bigger. For example, you can use TINYINT instead of INT to store smaller data. TINYINT can only hold values ranging from -128 to 127 compared to INT that holds values ranging from -2147483648 to 2147483647.

The size of the data type ranges from TINY, SMALL, MEDIUM, NORMAL, and BIG.

- TINYINT, SMALLINT, MEDIUMINT, INT, and BIGINT
- TINYBLOB, SMALLBLOB, MEDIUMBLOB, BLOB, and BIGBLOB
- TINYTEXT, SMALLTEXT, MEDIUMTEXT, TEXT, and BIGTEXT

You already know how to create databases and tables. Now, you need to learn how to insert values inside those tables.

INSERT INTO and VALUES

There are two ways to insert values in your database. Below is the syntax for the first method:

INSERT INTO <name of table>

VALUES (<value 1>, <value 2>, <value 3>);

The same result be done by:

INSERT INTO <name of table>

(<column 1>, <column 2>, <column 3>)

VALUES (<value 1>, <value 2>, <value 3>);

Take note that the first method will assign values according to the arrangement of your columns in the tables. In case you do not want to enter a data to one of the columns in your table, you will be forced to enter an empty value.

On the other hand, if you want full control of the INSERT operation, it will be much better to indicate the name of the corresponding columns that will be given data. Take note that the database will assign the values you will write with respect of the arrangement of the columns in your query.

For example, if you want to insert data in the example account table, you need to do this:

INSERT INTO account

(username, password, email, firstname, lastname)

VALUES

("Johnnyxxx", "123abc", "jjxxx@gmail.com, "Johnny", "Stew");

The statement will INSERT one entry to the database. You might have noticed that the example did not include a value for the ID field. You do not need to do that since the ID field has the AUTO_INCREMENT attribute. The database will be the one to generate a value to it.

SELECT and FROM

To check if the entry you sent was saved to the database, you can use SELECT. As mentioned before, the SELECT statement will retrieve all the data that you want from the database. Its syntax is:

SELECT <column 1> FROM <name of table>;

If you use this in the example account table and you want to get all the usernames in it, you can do it by:

SELECT username FROM account;

In case that you want to multiple records from two or more fields, you can do that by specifying another column. For example:

SELECT username, email FROM account;

WHERE

Unfortunately, using SELECT alone will provide you with tons of data. And you do not want that all the time. To filter out the results you want or to specify the data you want to receive, you can use the WHERE clause. For example:

SELECT <column 1> FROM <name of table>

WHERE <column> <operator> <value>;

If ever you need to get the username of all the people who have Johnny as their first name in the account table, you do that by:

SELECT username FROM account

WHERE firstname = "Johnny";

In the query above, the database will search all the records in the username column that has the value Johnny on the firstname column. The query will return Johnnyxxx and j_sasaki.

LIMIT

What if you only need a specific number of records to be returned? You can use the LIMIT clause for that. For example:

SELECT <column 1> FROM <name of table>

LIMIT <number>;

If you only want one record from the email column to be returned when you use SELECT on the account table, you can do it by:

SELECT email FROM account

LIMIT 1;

You can the LIMIT clause together with the WHERE clause for you to have a more defined search. For example:

SELECT username FROM account

WHERE firstname = "Johnny"

LIMIT 1;

Instead of returning two usernames that have Johnny in the firstname field, it will only return one.

UPDATE and SET

What if you made a mistake and you want to append an entry on your table? Well, you can use UPDATE for that. For example:

UPDATE <name of table>

SET <column 1>=<value 1>, <column 1>=<value 1>, <column 1>=<value 1>

WHERE <column> <operator> <value>;

In the example account table, if you want to change the name of all the people named Master to a different one, you can do that by:

UPDATE account

SET firstname="David"

WHERE firstname="Master";

Take note, you can perform an UPDATE without the WHERE clause. However, doing so will make the database think that you want to UPDATE all the records in the table. Remember that it is a bit complex to ROLLBACK changes in MySQL, so be careful.

DELETE

If you do not to remove an entire row, you can use DELETE. However, if you just want to delete or remove one piece of data in a column, it is better to use UPDATE and place a blank value instead. To perform a DELETE, follow this syntax:

```
DELETE FROM <name of table>

WHERE <column> <operator> <value>;
```

If you want to delete the first row in the account table, do this:

```
DELETE FROM account

WHERE id = 1;
```

Just like with the UPDATE statement, make sure that you use the WHERE clause when using DELETE. If not, all the rows in your table will disappear.

TRUNCATE TABLE

If you just want to remove all the data inside your table and keep all the settings that you have made to it you need to use TRUNCATE TABLE. This is the syntax for it:

```
TRUNCATE TABLE <name of table>;
```

If you want to do that to the account table, do this by entering:

```
TRUNCATE TABLE account;
```

DROP TABLE and DROP DATABASE

Finally, if you want to remove a table or database, you can use DROP. Below are examples on how to DROP the account table and sample database.

DROP TABLE account;

DROP DATABASE sample;

Chapter 5: MySQL and PHP

You already know how to manage a MySQL server to the most basic level. Now, it is time to use all those statements and use PHP to communicate with the MySQL server.

To interact or access a MySQL database, you need to send SQL queries to it. There are multiple ways you can do that. But if you want to do it in the web or your website, you will need to use a server side scripting language. And the best one to use is PHP.

In PHP, you can communicate to a MySQL server by using PDO (PHP Data Objects), MySQL extension, or MySQLi extension. Compared to MySQLi extension, PDO is a better choice when communicating with a MySQL database. However, in this book, only MySQLi extension will be discussed since it is less complex and easier to use.

Connecting to a MySQL database:

Before you can do or say anything to a MySQL server or a database, you will need to connect to it first. To do that, follow this example:

```
<?php
$dbservername = "localhost";
$dbusername = "YourDataBaseUserName";
$dbpassword = "YourPassword12345";

// Create a new connection object
$dbconnection = new mysqli($dbservername, $ dbusername, $ dbpassword);

// Check if connection was successful
if ($dbconnection->connect_error) {
  die("Connection failed/error: " . $dbconnection->connect_error);
}
echo "Connected successfully to database";
?>
```

In this example, you are using PHP's MySQLi to connect to your database. If you are going to test the code in the server that you installed in your computer, use localhost for your database's server name.

By the way, to prevent hackers on any random internet surfers to edit or access your databases, your MySQL server will require you to set a username and password. Every time you connect to it, you will need to include it to the parameters of the mysqli object.

In the example, you have created an object under the mysqli class. All the information that the server will send to you will be accessible in this object.

The third block of code is used to check if your connection request encountered any trouble. As you can see, the if statement is checking whether the connect_error property of the object $dbconnection contains a value. If it does, the code will be terminated and return an error message.

On the other hand, if the connect_error is null, the code will proceed and echo a message that will tell the user that the connection was successful.

Closing a connection

To close a mysqli object's connection, just invoke its close() method. For example:

```
$dbconnection->close();
```

Creating a new MySQL Database

```
<?php
$dbservername = "localhost";
$dbusername = "YourDataBaseUserName";
$dbpassword = "YourPassword12345";

// Create a new connection object
$dbconnection = new mysqli($dbservername, $ dbusername, $ dbpassword);

// Check if connection was successful
if ($dbconnection->connect_error) {
   die("Connection failed/error: " . $dbconnection->connect_error);
}


// Creating a Database

$dbSQL = "CREATE DATABASE YourDatabaseName";

if ($dbconnection->query($dbSQL) === TRUE) {

        echo "YourDatabaseName was created.";

}

else {

        echo "An error was encountered while creating your database: " .
$dbconnection->error;
```

```
}

$dbconnection->close();
?>
```

Before you request a database to be created, you must connect to your MySQL server first. Once you establish a connection, you will need to tell your server to create a database by sending an SQL query.

The $dbSQL variable was created to hold the query string that you will send. You do not need to do this, but creating a variable for your queries is good practice since it will make your code more readable. If you did not create a variable holder for your SQL, you can still create a database by:

```
$dbconnection->query("CREATE DATABASE YourDatabaseName")
```

The if statement was used to both execute the query method of $dbconnection and to check if your server will be able to do it. If it does, it will return a value of TRUE. The if statement will inform you that you were able to create your database.

On the other hand, if it returns false or an error instead, the example code will return a message together with the error.

Once the database was created, the connection was closed.

Interacting with a Database

Once you create a database, you can now send SQL queries and do some operations in it. Before you do that, you need to connect to the server and then specify the name of the database, which you want to interact with, in the parameters of the mysqli class when creating a mysqli object. For example:

```
<?php
$dbservername = "localhost";
$dbusername = "YourDataBaseUserName";
$dbpassword = "YourPassword12345";

$dbname = "sample"

// Create a new connection object
$dbconnection = new mysqli($dbservername, $ dbusername, $ dbpassword, $sample);

// Check if connection was successful
if ($dbconnection->connect_error) {
  die("Connection failed/error: " . $dbconnection->connect_error);
}
```

```
echo "Connected successfully to database";
?>
```

phpMyAdmin

In case you do not want to rely on code to create and manage your databases, you can use the phpMyAdmin tool. Instead of relying on sending SQL queries, you will be given a user interface that is easier to use and reduces the chances of error since you do not need to type SQL and create typos. Think of it as Microsoft Access with a different interface.

The tool will also allow you to enter SQL if you want to and it will provide you with the SQL queries that it has used to perform the requests you make. Due to that, this tool will help you get more familiar with SQL. And the best thing about it is that it is free.

On the other hand, you can use phpMyAdmin to check the changes you made to the database while you are studying MySQL. If you do that, you will be able to debug faster since you do not need to redisplay or create a code for checking the contents of your database using PHP.

Conclusion

Thank you again for purchasing this book!

I hope this book was able to help you to master the fundamentals of MySQL programming.

The next step is to learn more about:

- Advanced SQL Statements and Clauses
- Attributes
- The MySQLi Class
- PHP Data Object
- Security Measures in MySQL
- Importing and Exporting MySQL Databases
- Different Applications of MySQL

Those topics will advance your MySQL programming skills. Well, even with the things you have learned here, you will already be capable of doing great things. With the knowledge you have, you can already create an online chat application, social network site, and online games!

That is no exaggeration. If you do not believe that, well, check out the sample codes that experts share on the web. You will be surprised how simple their codes are.

Finally, if you enjoyed this book, please take the time to share your thoughts and post a review on Amazon. We do our best to reach out to readers and provide the best value we can. Your positive review will help us achieve that. It'd be greatly appreciated!

Thank you and good luck!

Check Out My Other Books

Below you'll find some of my other popular books that are popular on Amazon and Kindle as well. Simply click on the links below to check them out. Alternatively, you can visit my author page on Amazon to see other work done by me.

Android Programming in a Day

Python Programming in a Day

C Programming Success in a Day

C Programming Professional Made Easy

JavaScript Programming Made Easy

PHP Programming Professional Made Easy

C ++ Programming Success in a Day

Windows 8 Tips for Beginners

HTML Professional Programming Made Easy

If the links do not work, for whatever reason, you can simply search for these titles on the Amazon website to find them.

www.ingramcontent.com/pod-product-compliance
Lightning Source LLC
Chambersburg PA
CBHW061043050326
40689CB00012B/2957